# really easy piano

T0084201

# QUEEN

ISBN: 978-1-5400-4811-0

**HAL•LEONARD®**

Visit Hal Leonard Online at
**www.halleonard.com**

Contact us:
**Hal Leonard**
7777 West Bluemound Road
Milwaukee, WI 53213
Email: info@halleonard.com

In Europe, contact:
**Hal Leonard Europe Limited**
42 Wigmore Street
Marylebone, London, W1U 2RY
Email: info@halleonardeurope.com

In Australia, contact:
**Hal Leonard Australia Pty. Ltd.**
4 Lentara Court
Cheltenham, Victoria, 3192 Australia
Email: info@halleonard.com.au

# QUEEN

# QUEEN

# Another One Bites The Dust

### Words & Music by John Deacon

This single from Queen was written by bass player, John Deacon, and released in 1980 as part of their album of the same year, *The Game*. A nod to the disco style is apparent in this track, as Deacon explains how he was influenced by Chic's single, 'Good Times'. Originally, the band did not consider releasing it as a single until music mogul Michael Jackson convinced them to do just that!

**Hints & Tips:** Practice the syncopation in the chorus a few times so you grasp the rhythm.
The left-hand sixteenth note should sound at exactly the same time as the right-hand sixteenth note.

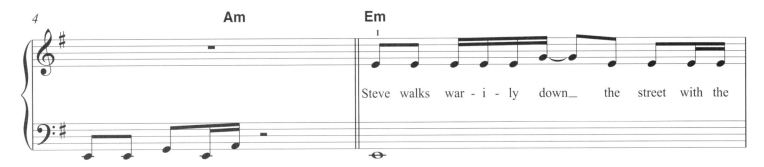

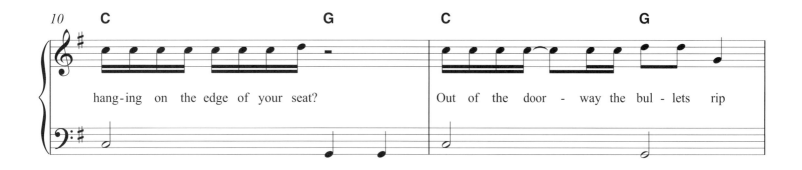

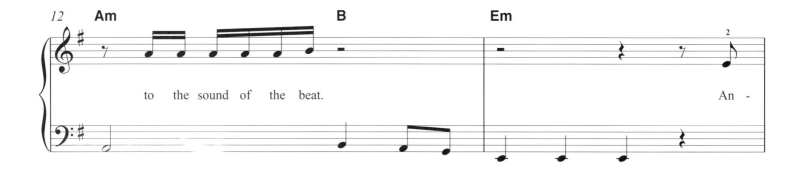

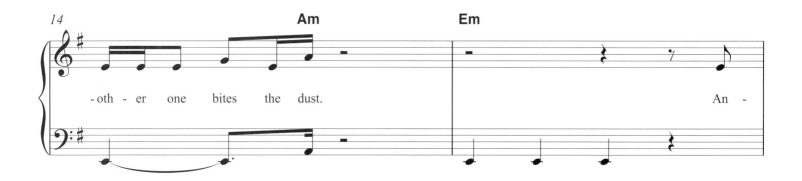

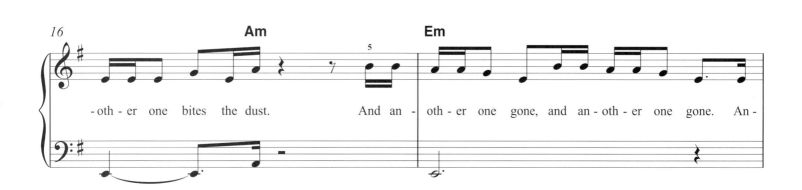

-oth - er one bites the dust.

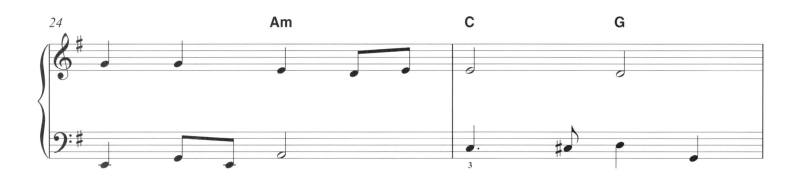

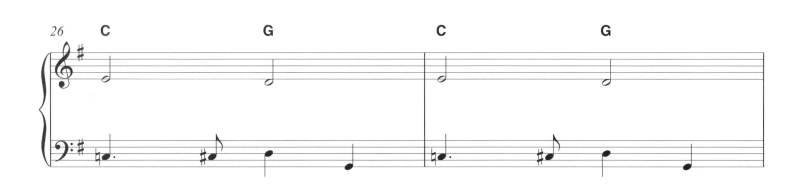

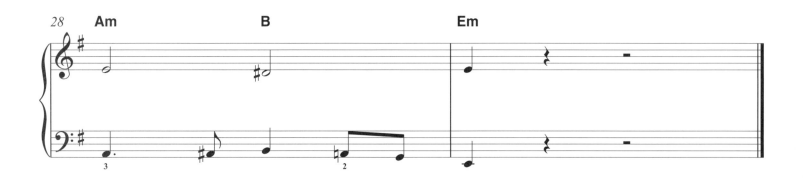

# Bohemian Rhapsody

### Words & Music by Freddie Mercury

The first song ever to reach to No. 1 twice with the same version, winner of just about every musical award there is, and one of only two contemporary tracks to make it into the UK's Desert Island Discs Top 8, this internationally-acclaimed work of genius can justifiably claim to be the most revered six minutes in the history of rock music.

**Hints & Tips: Note the time signature changes at the beginning.**
**Bring out the harmonies at the start as they play a big part in the feel of the song.**
**Play through the passages with accidentals thoroughly as some of these are quite tricky.**

**Fairly free tempo** ♩ = 72

Is this the real life? Is this just fan-ta-sy?

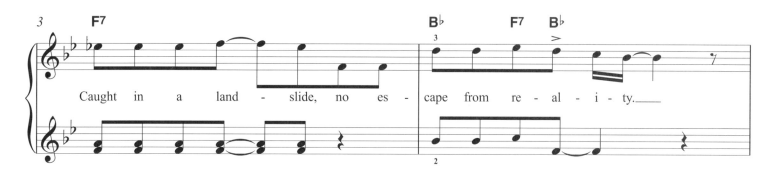

Caught in a land-slide, no es-cape from re-al-i-ty.

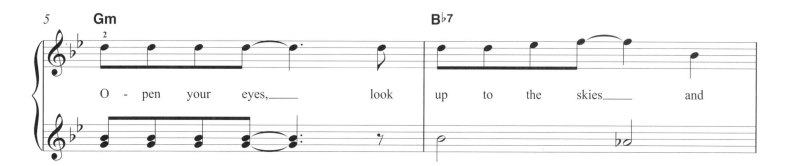

O-pen your eyes, look up to the skies and

see. I'm just a poor boy, I need no sym-path-y 'cause I'm

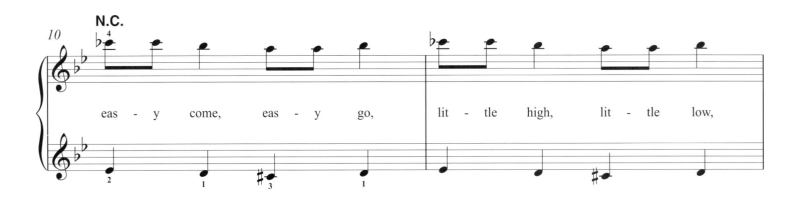

easy come, easy go, little high, little low,

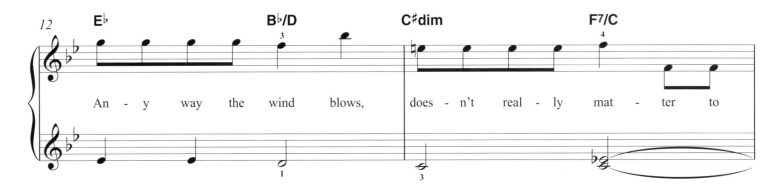

Any way the wind blows, does-n't real-ly mat-ter to

me, to___ me.

Ma - ma,___ just killed a man,___ put a gun a-gainst___ his head,___ pulled my

trig - ger, now___ he's dead.__ Ma - ma,___ life had just be-gun but

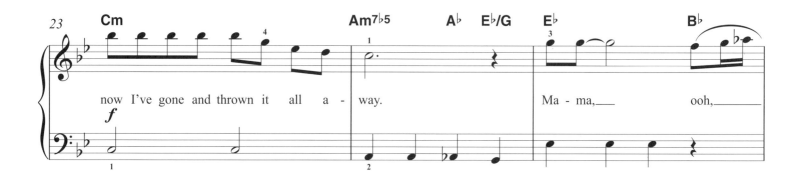

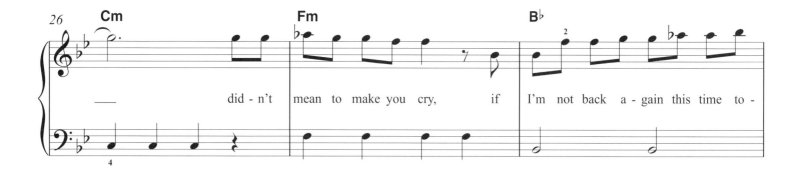

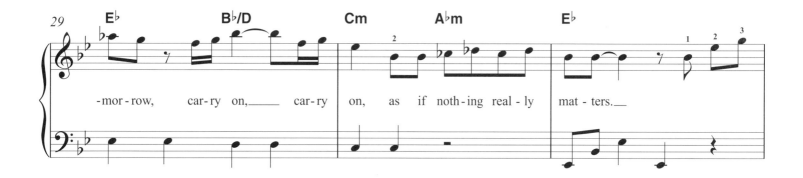

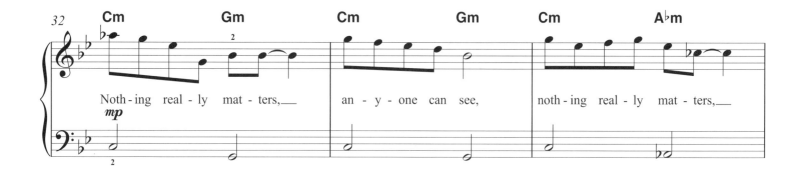

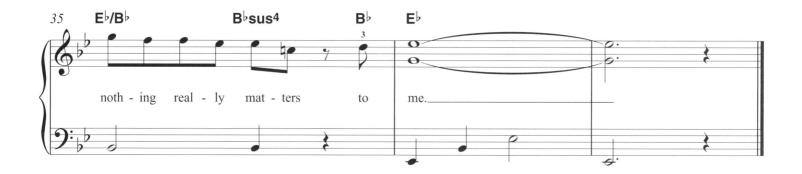

# Breakthru

**Words & Music by Freddie Mercury, Brian May, Roger Taylor and John Deacon**

The rapid rhythmic beat of this song is strongly reminiscent of a steam train thundering along the tracks.
So, in the video that accompanied its release as a single, shot on the Nene Valley Railway near
Cambridge, the band perform onboard an old locomotive, renamed The Miracle Express.

**Hints & Tips: Keep the driving quarter notes going steadily throughout to maintain the pace.**

**Fast, with strong beat** ♩ = 180

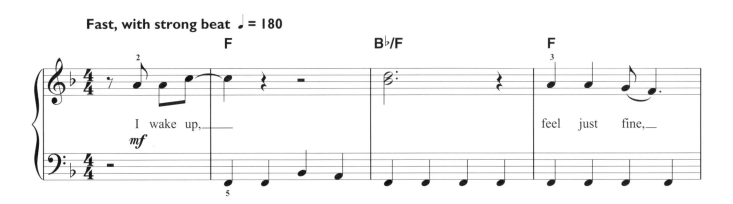

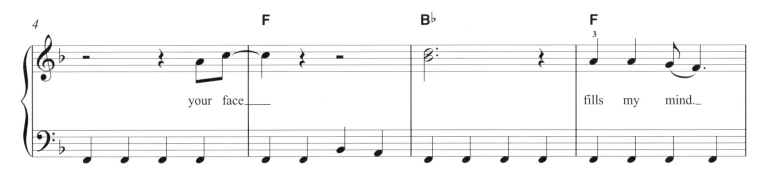

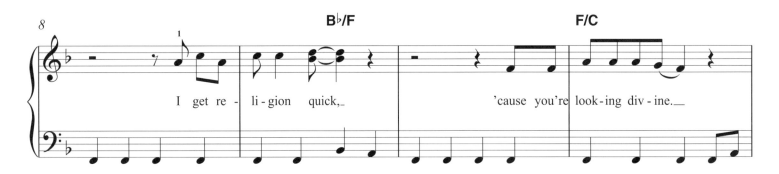

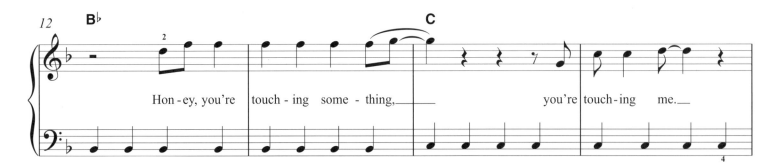

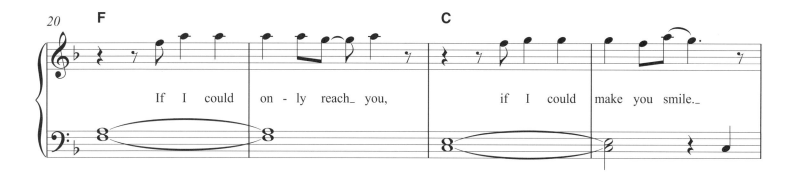

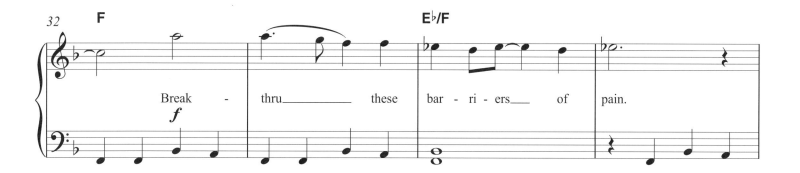

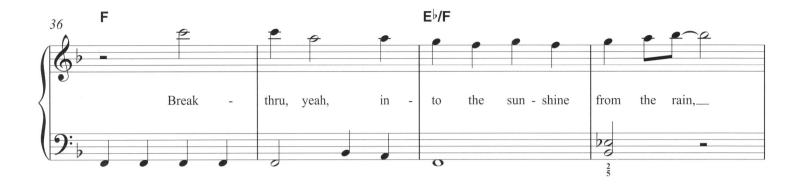

Break - thru, yeah, in - to the sun - shine from the rain,___

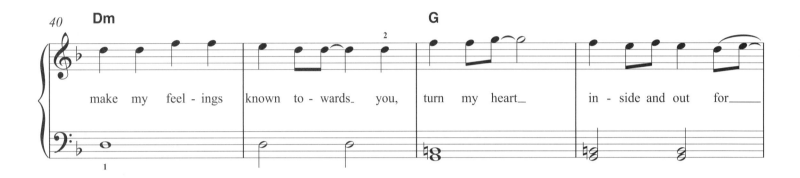

make my feel - ings known to - wards___ you, turn my heart___ in - side and out for_____

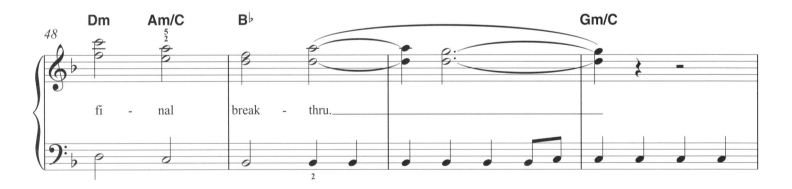

___ you now. Some - how_____ I have to make this

fi - nal break - thru._____

Now!

# Crazy Little Thing Called Love

### Words & Music by Freddie Mercury

Allegedly composed by Freddie Mercury whilst having a bath, in 1980 it became Queen's first No. 1 single in the USA. *The Game*, the album on which it featured, was the first Queen album to be released on CD, their first to reach No. 1 in the US and the first to use synthesizers, as the band adopted the bass-driven grooves of the day.

**Hints & Tips:** Keep both hands light throughout. Look through the piece carefully before playing to make sure you know where all the accidentals are. Count through bars 33–36, making sure full value is given to the rests in between the triplets.

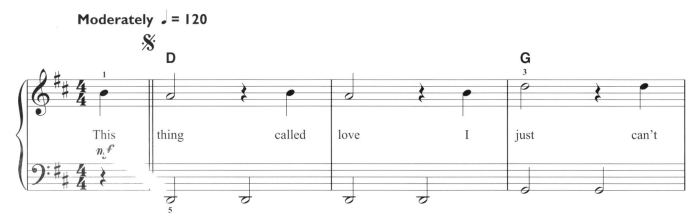

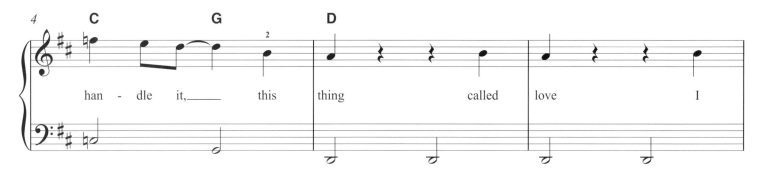

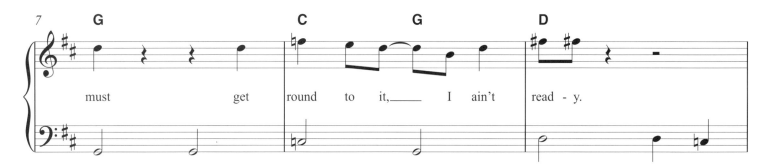

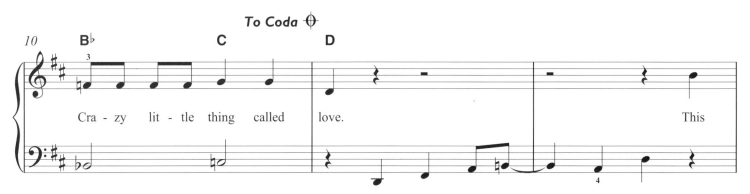

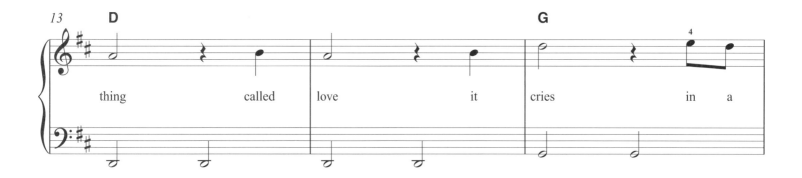

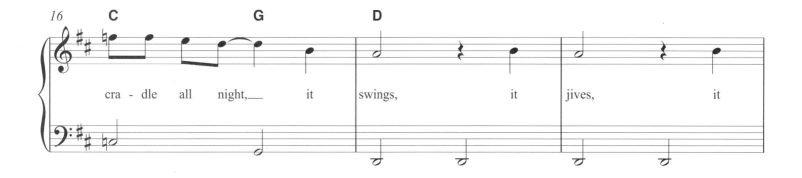

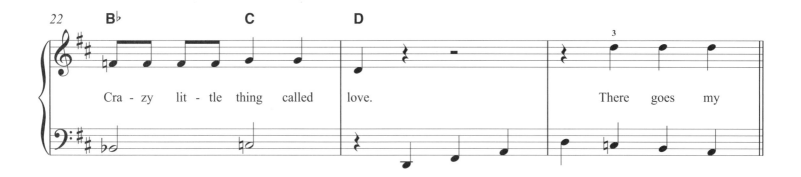

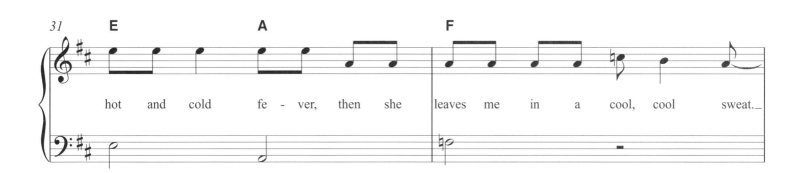

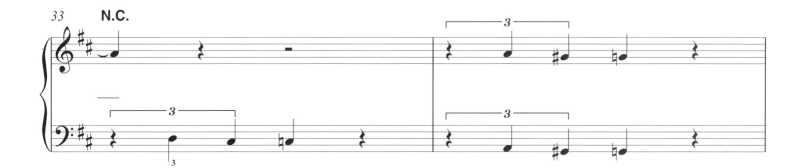

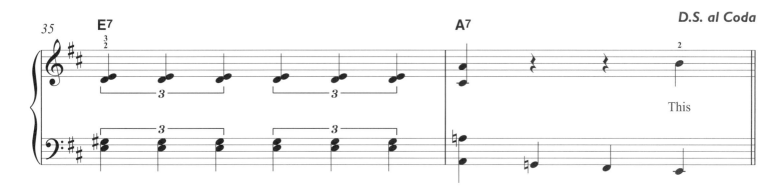

# Don't Stop Me Now

**Words & Music by Freddie Mercury**

The first Queen single released on a cassette tape, this song has become one of the most frequently covered. A version by McFly, which was the official song for *Sport Relief 2006*, reached No. 1 in the UK Singles Chart in July, a year after being voted 'The Greatest Driving Song Ever' by viewers of the BBC TV programme *Top Gear*.

**Hints & Tips:** This song is quite fast, so start off by practicing it slowly and build up speed once you're more confident. There are some big stretches in the melody, so take the time to look at the fingering.

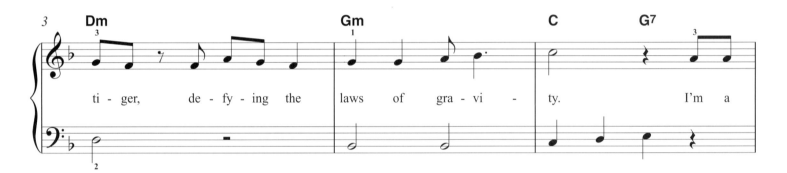

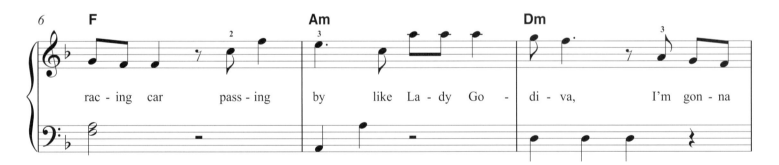

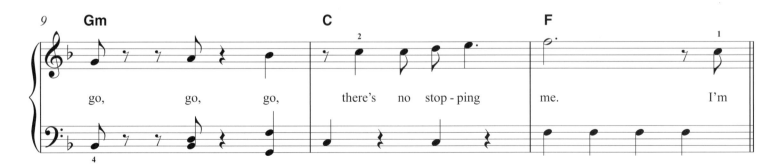

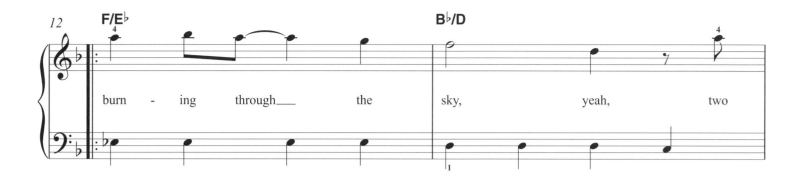

burn - ing through___ the sky, yeah, two

hun - dred de - grees___ that's why they call me Mis - ter Fah - ren -

-heit. I'm trav -'ling at the speed of light, I wan - na make a

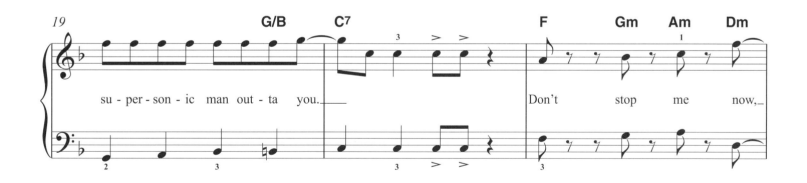

su - per - son - ic man out - ta you.___ Don't stop me now,___

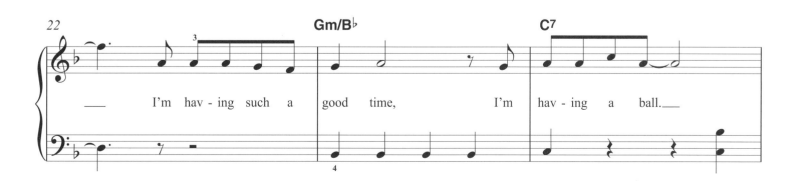

___ I'm hav - ing such a good time, I'm hav - ing a ball.___

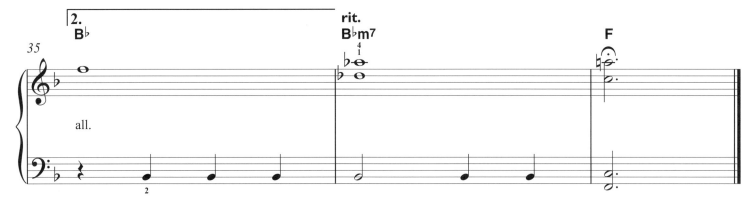

# I Want It All

Words & Music by Freddie Mercury, Brian May, Roger Taylor and John Deacon

Despite songwriter Brian May claiming that it is merely about having ambitions and fighting for one's own goals,
featuring themes of rebellion and social upheaval, this heavy rock number from *The Miracle*, Queen's sixth UK
No. 1 album, became an anti-apartheid song in South Africa and a rallying anthem for African-American youth.

**Hints & Tips:** The melody in the right hand has a few leaps; be aware
of where these are and make sure your hand is in the correct position.

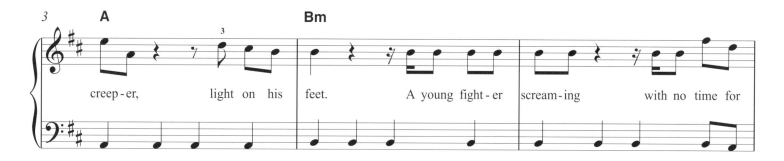

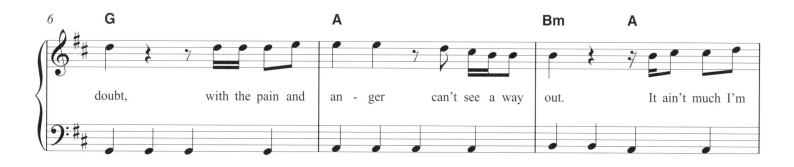

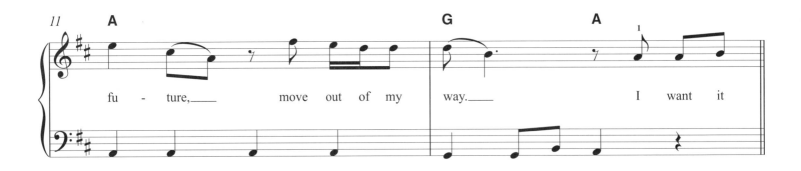

fu - ture,____ move out of my way.____ I want it

all, I want it all, I want it all, and I want it

now. I want it all, I want it all, I want it

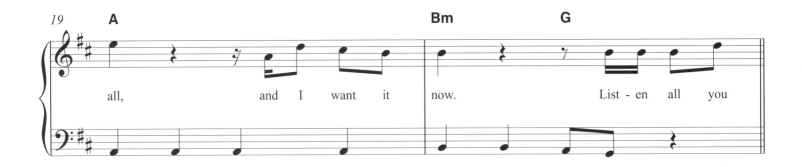

all, and I want it now. List - en all you

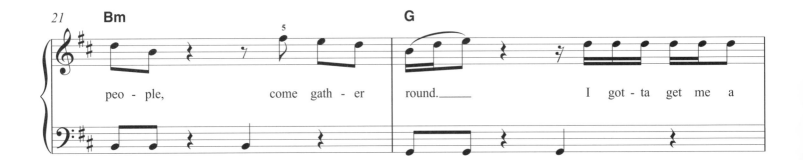

peo - ple, come gath - er round.____ I got - ta get me a

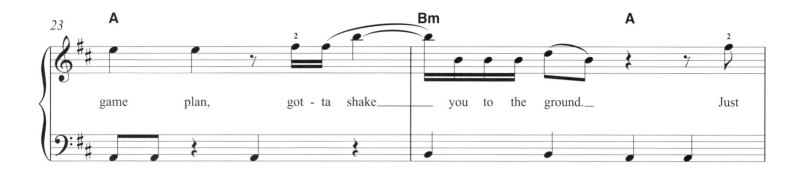

game plan, got-ta shake____ you to the ground.____ Just

give me, what I know is mine, peo-ple do you hear me? Just

give me the sign.____ It ain't much I'm ask - ing, if you want the

D.S. al Coda

truth, here's to the fu - ture____ for the dreams of youth. I want it

𝄋 Coda

all. And I want it now.

23

# I Want To Break Free

**Words & Music by John Deacon**

Written in 1983 by bassist John Deacon and influenced by prevailing men's attitudes to the women's liberation movement, this song came to be regarded as an anthem for the fight against oppression. Its original music video featured the band dressed in women's clothes in a parody of the long-running soap, *Coronation Street*.

**Hints & Tips: There are a lot of triplets in this song, so take care they are not rushed and make them nice and even.**

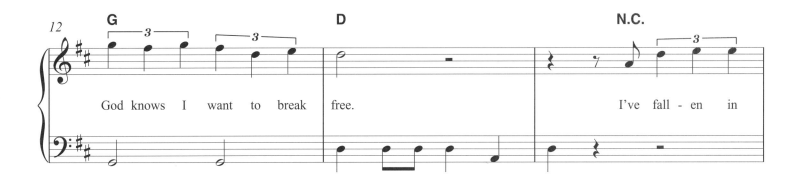

G            D            N.C.

God knows I want to break free.      I've fall - en in

D

love,___      I've fall - en in love for the first time and

G

this time I know it's for real.___      I've fall - en in

D                                      A

love.___     Yeah.           God    knows,___

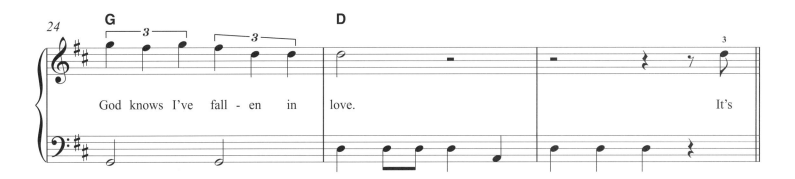

G                    D

God knows I've fall - en in love.               It's

strange but it's true,___ hey, I can't get o - ver the way you

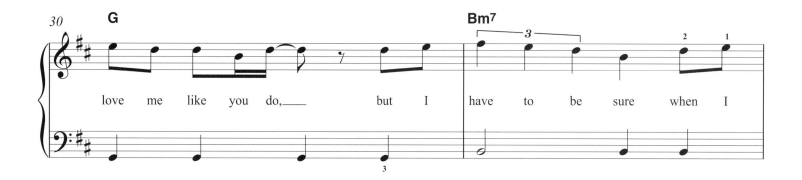

love me like you do,___ but I have to be sure when I

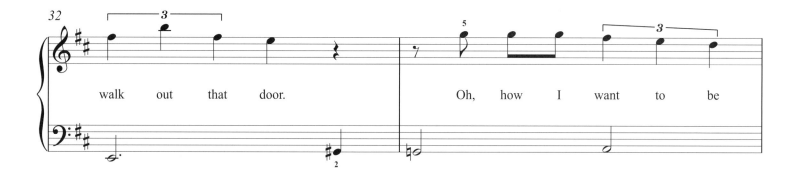

walk out that door. Oh, how I want to be

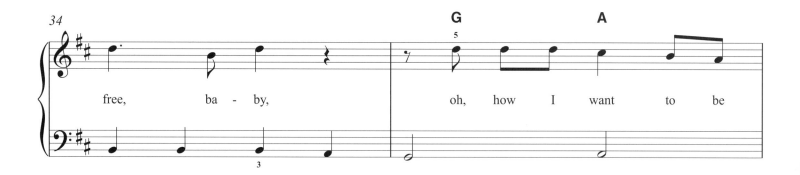

free, ba - by, oh, how I want to be

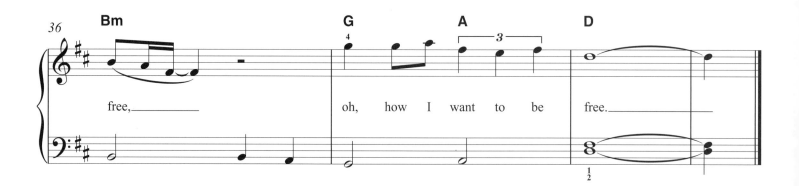

free,___ oh, how I want to be free.___

# Killer Queen

### Words & Music by Freddie Mercury

As disclosed by Freddie Mercury, this song is about 'a high class call girl'. From their 1974 album, *Sheer Heart Attack*, this track was Queen's first major breakthrough into the worldwide singles charts. The most famous line from the song is, 'let them eat cake, she says, just like Marie Antoinette', as it refers to the legend that Marie Antoinette — the last Queen of France before the French Revolution — made this insensitive remark upon hearing that the peasants had no bread to eat.

**Hints & Tips:** Take care over the changes of time signature throughout this song. Practice these passages several times to get a hang of them, using a metronome and counting out the quarter notes if useful.

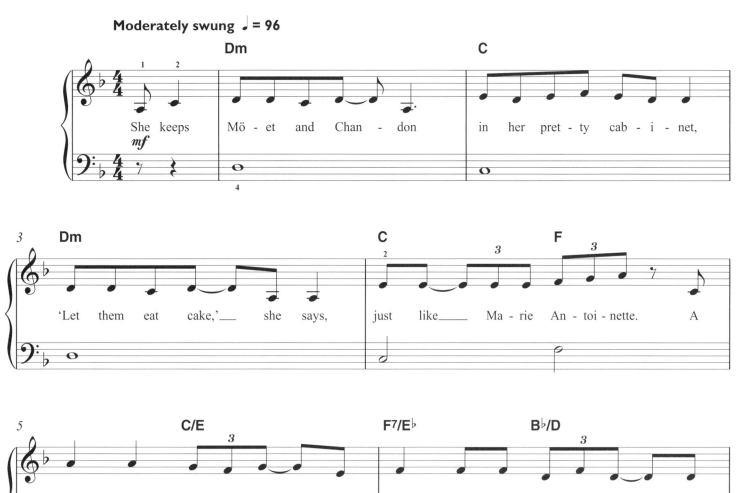

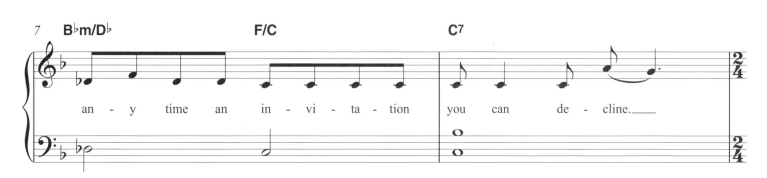

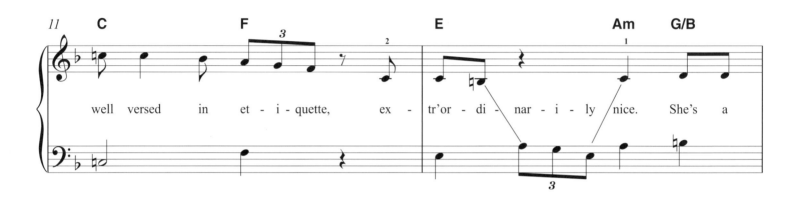

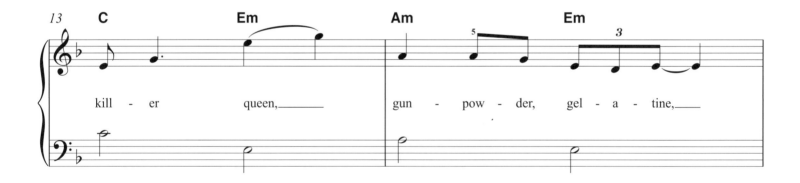

mind,___ an - y time,___ ooh. Re - com - mend - ed at the price,___ in -

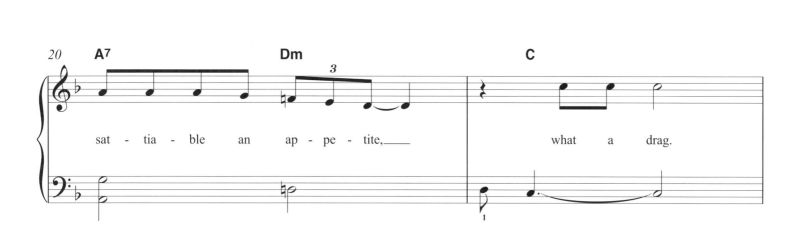

sat - tia - ble an ap - pe - tite,_____ what a drag.

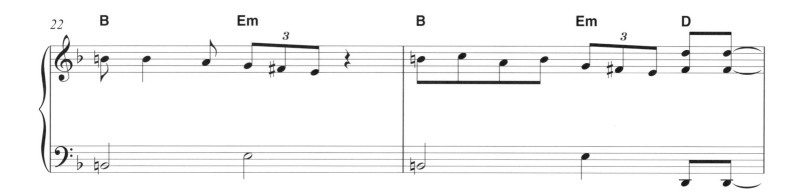

# A Kind Of Magic

**Words & Music by Roger Taylor**

On the basis of their strong, anthemic songs, in 1985 Queen were commissioned to compose music for the soundtrack of the movie *Highlander*. This project expanded into their 12th studio album *A Kind Of Magic*, which includes this song by Roger Taylor, the lyrics of which make several references to snippets from the film's script.

**Hints & Tips: Keep the left hand at a constant and steady beat throughout. Don't let this overpower the melody, but bring it out whenever the left hand has the eighth-note patterns which mimic the tune.**

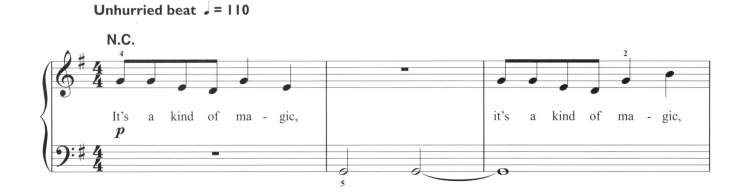

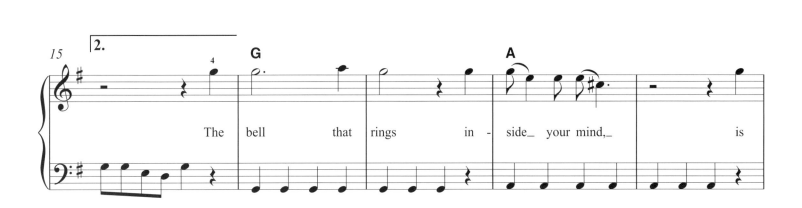

The bell that rings in - side__ your mind,__ is

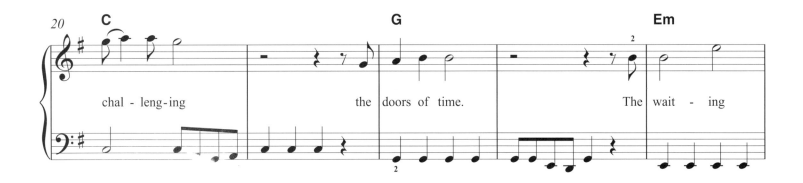

chal - leng-ing the doors of time. The wait - ing

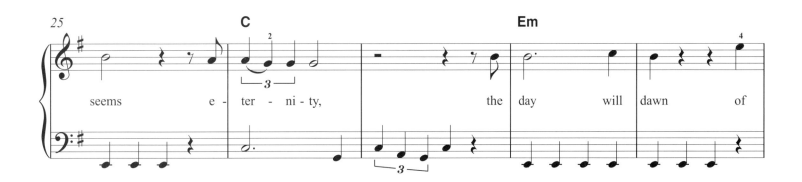

seems e - ter - ni - ty, the day will dawn of

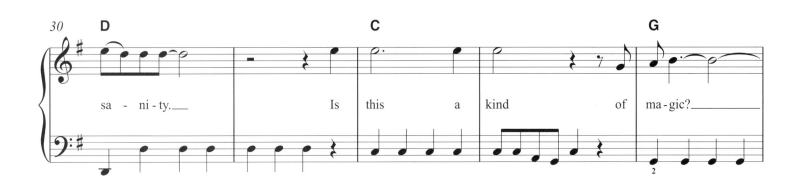

sa - ni - ty.__ Is this a kind of ma-gic?__

**Slower**

# Radio Ga Ga

**Words & Music by Roger Taylor**

Written by Queen's drummer, Roger Taylor, this song was inspired by a comment made by his infant son on hearing something which he didn't like on the radio. The lyrics reference two important radio events; a 1938 broadcast by Orson Welles and Winston Churchill's 'This was their finest hour' wartime speech from June 1940.

**Hints & Tips: Keep the beat strong and steady in this one and be wary of accidentals.**

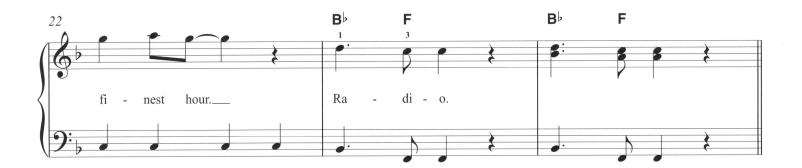

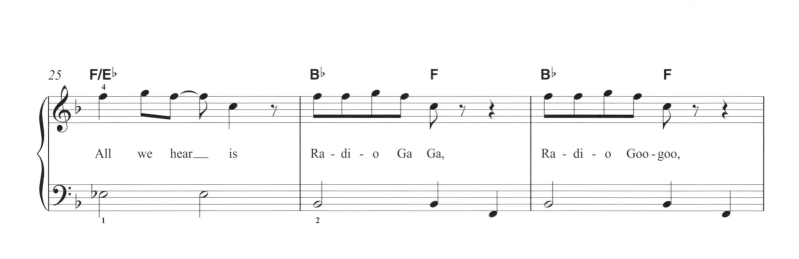

All we hear__ is Ra - di - o Ga Ga, Ra - di - o Goo - goo,

Ra - di - o Ga Ga. All we hear__ is Ra - di - o Ga Ga

Ra - di - o Bla - bla. Ra - di - o_____ what's new?___

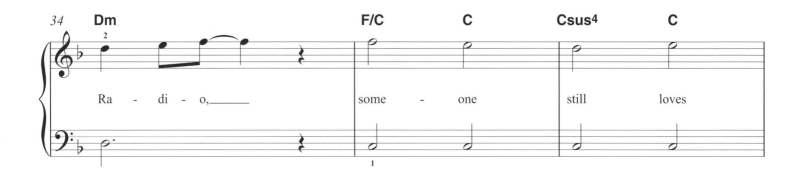

Ra - di - o,_____ some - one still loves

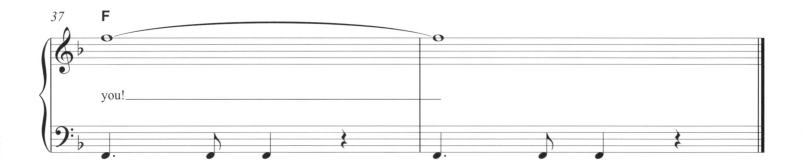

you!_____

# Save Me

### Words & Music by Brian May

This rock ballad was written by Queen's virtuoso guitarist, Brian May, about a friend whose relationship had ended. In recent years May returned to post-graduate studies in astrophysics, for which he was awarded a PhD by Imperial College, London in 2008, completion of his thesis coming 30 years after he started his research.

**Hints & Tips:** Starting off softly and slowly, this song changes key for a contrasting chorus, which should be played louder. Bars 23 & 28 should be played through slowly to make sure you've got the hang of the rhythm, fingering and accidentals.

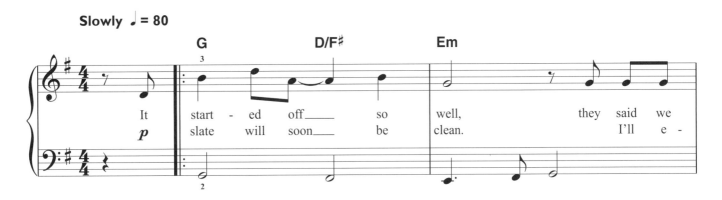

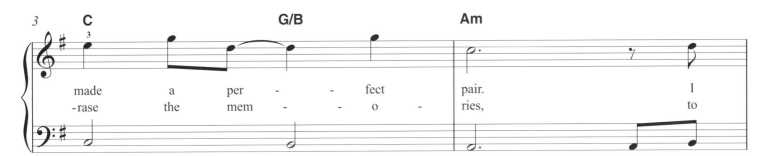

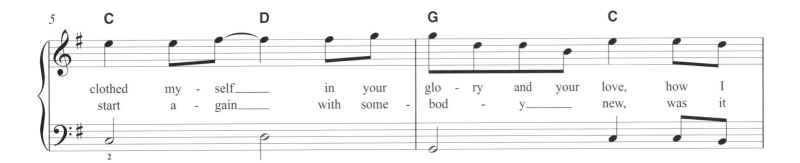

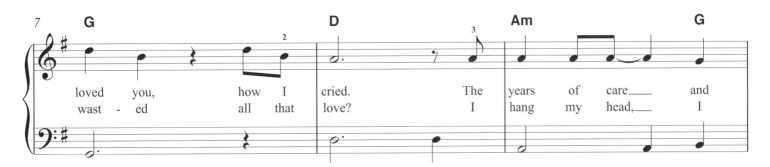

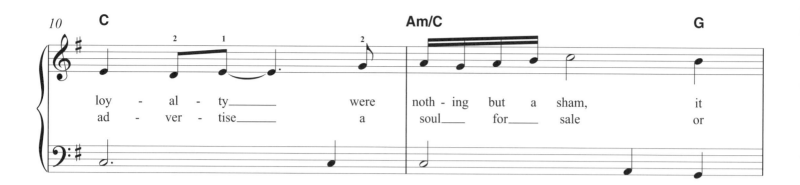

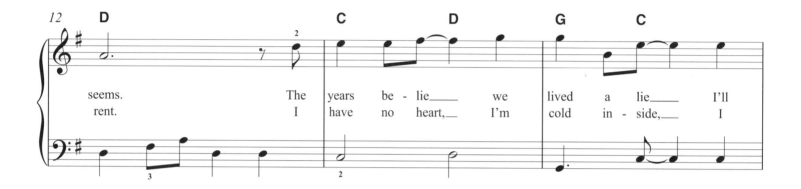

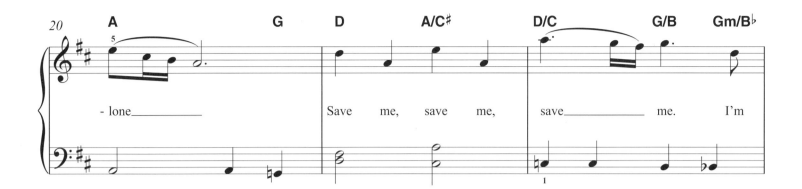

-lone_____ Save me, save me, save_____ me. I'm

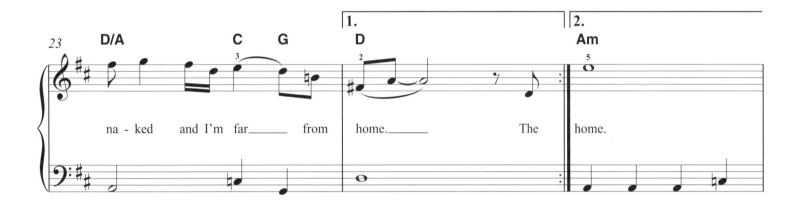

na - ked and I'm far_____ from home._____ The home.

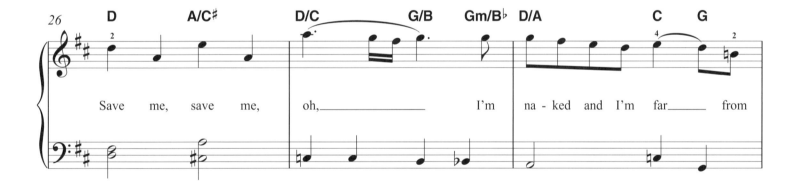

Save me, save me, oh,_____ I'm na - ked and I'm far_____ from

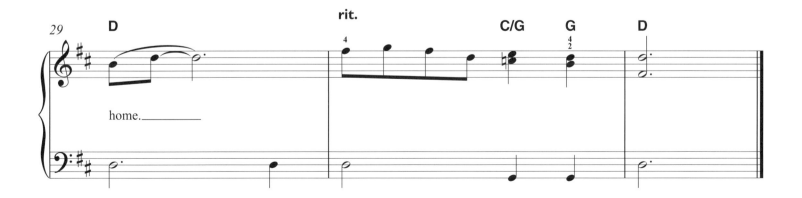

home._____

# Seven Seas Of Rhye

### Words & Music by Freddie Mercury

Taken from their second album, *Queen II*, this song was rush-released following the band's appearance on *Top of the Pops* and in 1974 became their first major singles-chart hit. Inspired by a photo of Marlene Dietrich, the iconic monochromatic image of them on the LP's cover was echoed by it having a Side White and a Side Black.

**Hints & Tips:** Be careful of the accidentals from bar 14 onwards. Watch out for the high F♯ in bar 20; the long D in the bar before should give you plenty of time to make sure you land on the correct note!

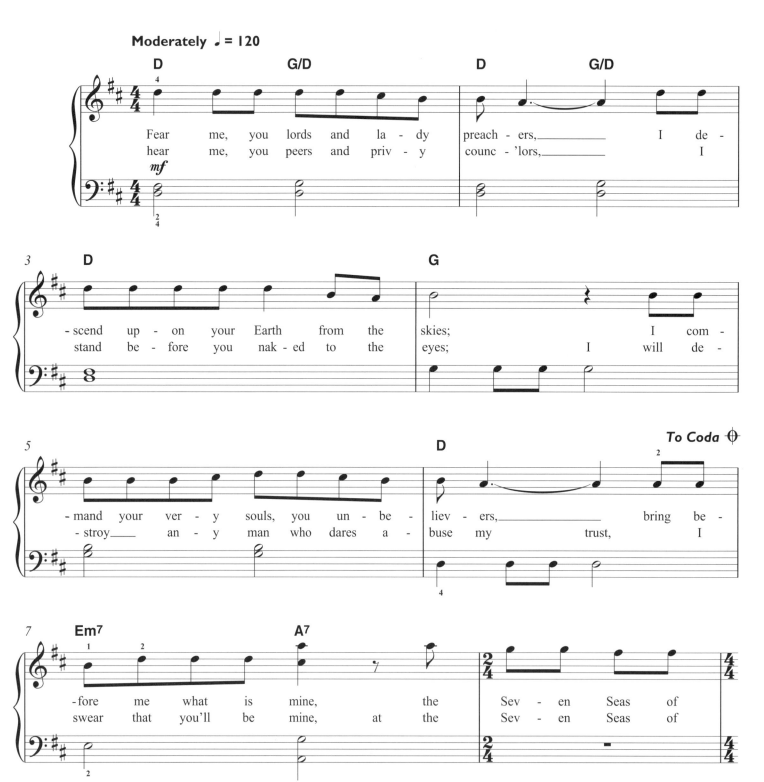

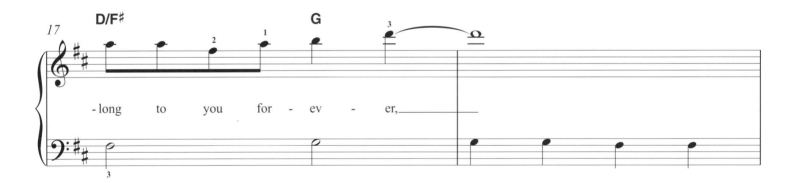

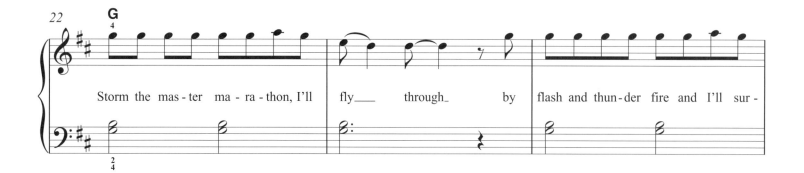

Storm the mas-ter ma-ra-thon, I'll fly___ through___ by flash and thun-der fire and I'll sur-

-vive, I'll sur-vive, I'll sur-vive, then I'll de-fy the laws of

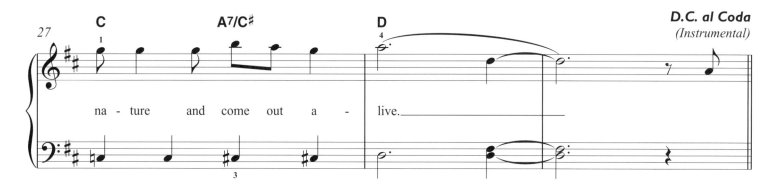

*D.C. al Coda*
*(Instrumental)*

na-ture and come out a-live.___

⊕ *Coda*

I'll take you to the Sev-en Seas of

Rhye.

# The Show Must Go On

**Words & Music by Freddie Mercury, Brian May, Roger Taylor and John Deacon**

Facing his impending death, although Freddie Mercury was too ill to make live appearances, he was not too ill to record and this song is about his continuing efforts to do so, despite his deteriorating health. Issued as a single in October 1991, it proved to be the last that Queen released before Freddie's death just six weeks later.

**Hints & Tips:** The right-hand eighth notes at the start should be played lightly, almost *staccato*.
Go through the fingering of the melody so you know when to change your hand position.

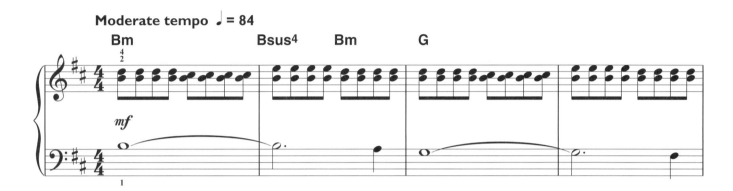

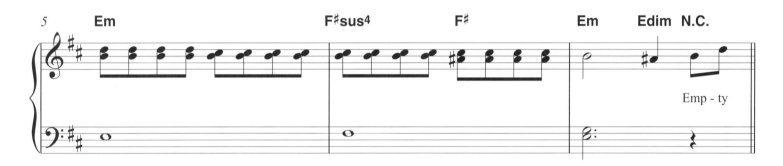

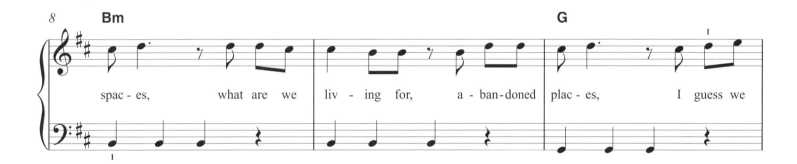

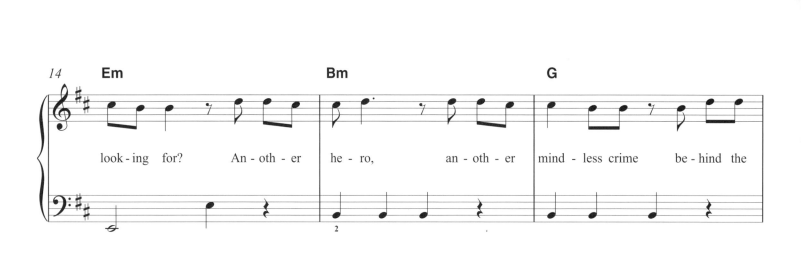

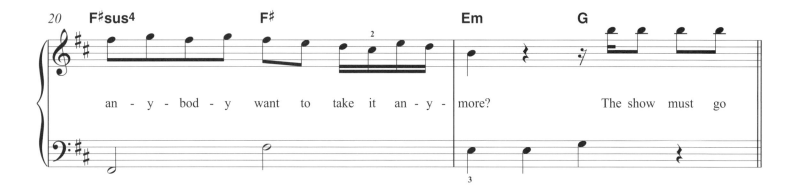

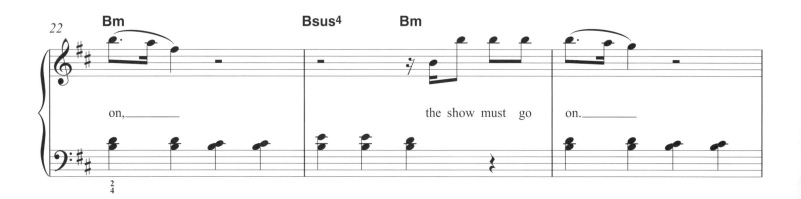

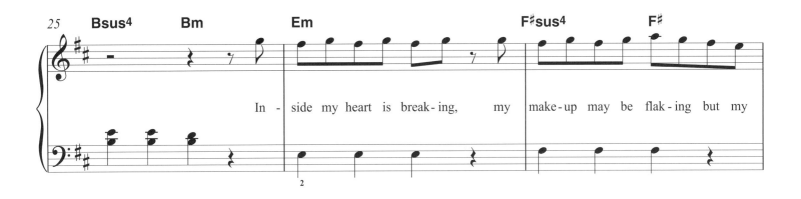

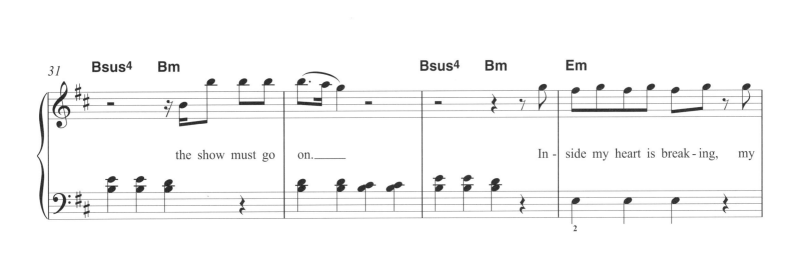

# Somebody To Love

Words & Music by Freddie Mercury

The soul-searching lyrics of this song, the biggest-selling single from the album *A Day At The Races*, are about faith, with the singer questioning the lack of love in his life and the existence of God. The recording seemed to feature a large gospel choir, although layered vocal tracks enabled this to be achieved by just three voices.

**Hints & Tips:** Play through the right hand on its own a few times first until you're confident with it, as it's quite tricky in places. Note where the changes of time signature are so that the piece flows nicely all the way through.

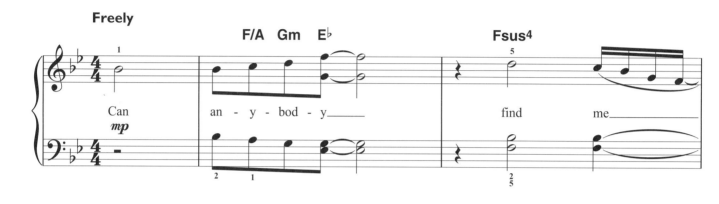

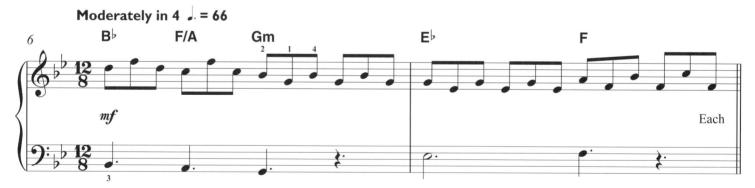

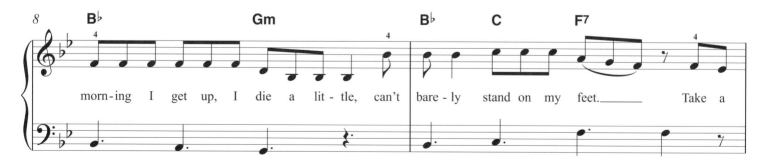

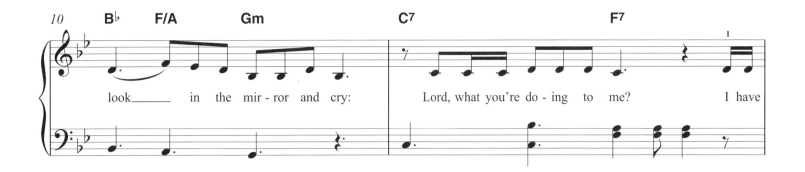

look_____ in the mir-ror and cry: Lord, what you're do-ing to me? I have

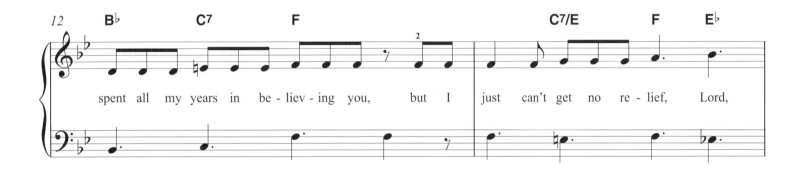

spent all my years in be - liev - ing you, but I just can't get no re - lief, Lord,

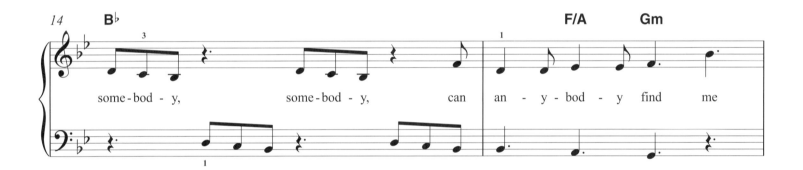

some-bod - y, some-bod - y, can an - y-bod - y find me

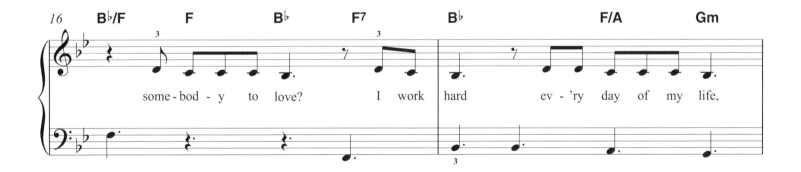

some - bod - y to love? I work hard ev - 'ry day of my life,

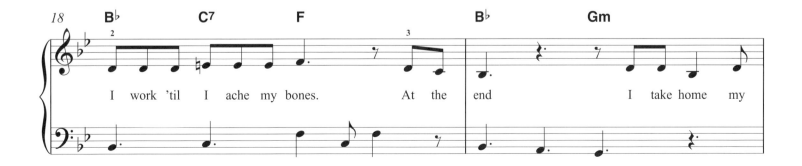

I work 'til I ache my bones. At the end I take home my

hard earned pay all on my own. I get down on my knees and I start to pray 'til the

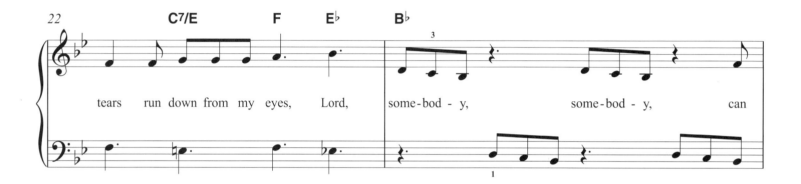

tears run down from my eyes, Lord, some-bod - y, some-bod - y, can

an - y-bod - y find me some-bod - y to love?

# Too Much Love Will Kill You

Words & Music by Brian May, Elizabeth Lamers and Frank Musker

After Freddie Mercury's death in 1991, the remaining band members worked on a new project with the vocal recordings that he had left behind and in 1995 produced the album *Made In Heaven*, which features this song. Originally recorded as early as in 1988, it won the 1997 Novello Award for Best Song Musically and Lyrically.

**Hints & Tips: Make the most of the melody in this; it should be played very expressively.**

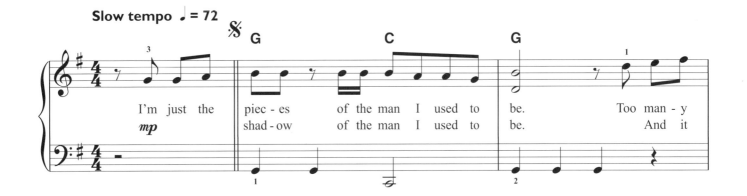

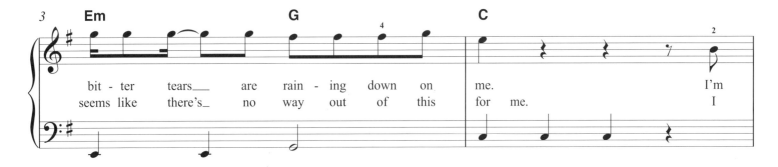

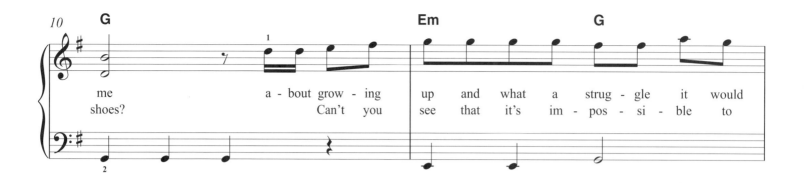

me
shoes?
a - bout grow - ing
Can't you
up and what a strug - gle it would
see that it's im - pos - si - ble to

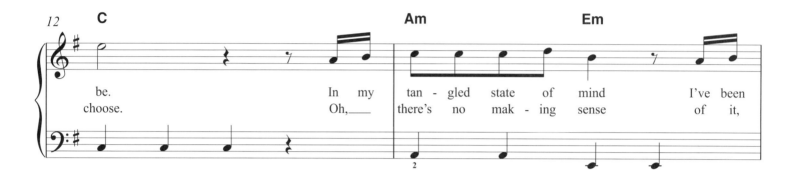

be.
choose.
In my
Oh,____
tan - gled state of mind
there's no mak - ing sense
I've been
of it,

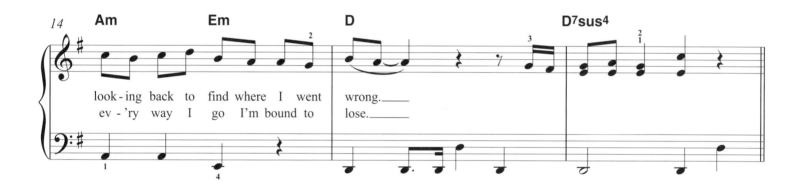

look - ing back to find where I went
ev - 'ry way I go I'm bound to
wrong.____
lose.____

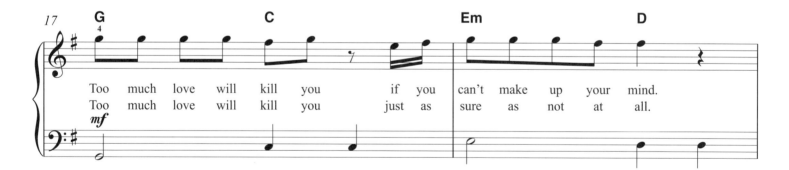

Too much love will kill you
Too much love will kill you
if you
just as
can't make up your mind.
sure as not at all.

Torn be - tween the lov - er
Drain the pow - er that's in you,
and the
make you
love you leave be - hind.____
plead and scream and crawl.____
You're
The

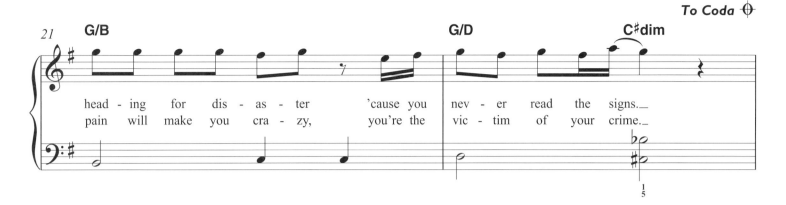

head - ing for dis - as - ter 'cause you nev - er read the signs.__
pain will make you cra - zy, you're the vic - tim of your crime.__

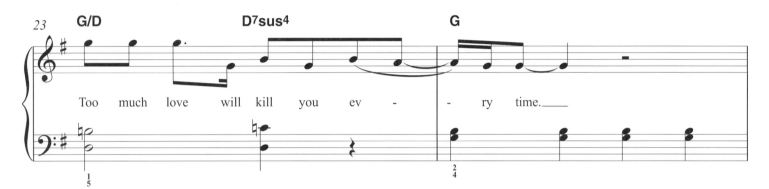

Too much love will kill you ev - - ry time.____

I'm just the

⊕ *Coda*

Too much love will kill you__ in__ the end,

In__ the end.__

# Under Pressure

**Words & Music by Freddie Mercury, John Deacon, Brian May, Roger Taylor and David Bowie**

Memorable for John Deacon's distinctive bass line, this song came about from a collaboration between the band and David Bowie, who in 1981 was recording at the same studios in Montreux, Switzerland. They probably could not have imagined that their late night jam session would turn out to be an international No. 1 smash hit.

**Hints & Tips:** There are some tricky right-hand rhythms in this one; play the hands through separately until you've got the hang of them before trying hands together.

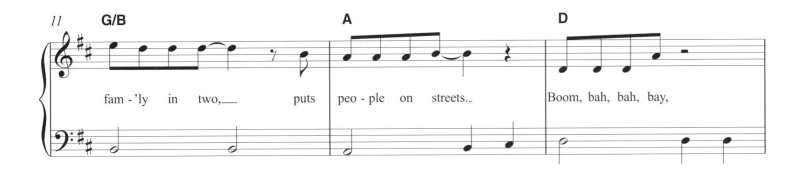

fam - 'ly in two,___ puts peo - ple on streets.__ Boom, bah, bah, bay,

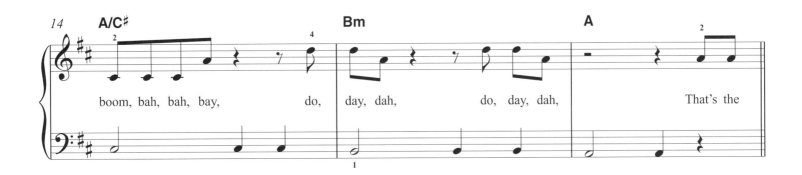

boom, bah, bah, bay, do, day, dah, do, day, dah, That's the

ter - ror of know - ing what this world is a - bout.

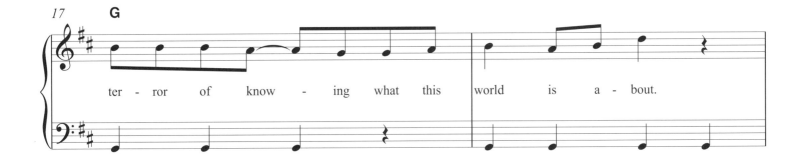

Watch - ing some good friends scream - ing, 'Let me out!'___ Pray to -

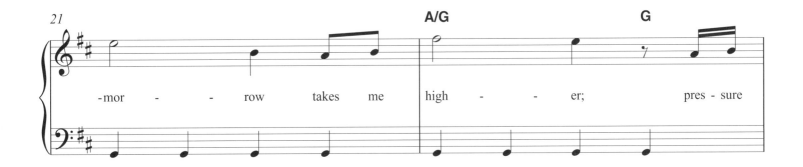

-mor - - row takes me high - - er; pres - sure

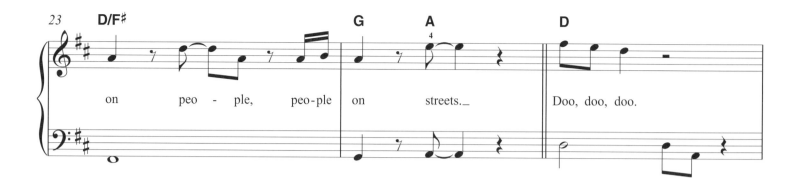

on peo - ple, peo-ple on streets.___ Doo, doo, doo.

Ba, da, ba, ba, ba. O. K.___

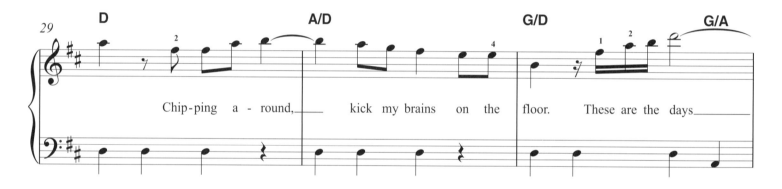

Chip-ping a - round,___ kick my brains on the floor. These are the days___

___ it nev - er rains but it pours.___

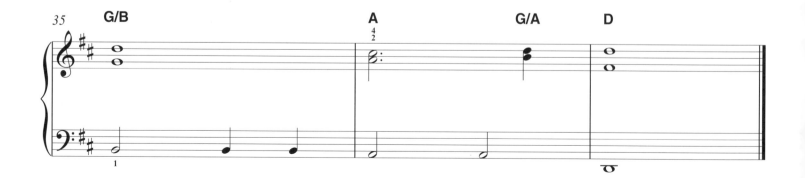

# Who Wants To Live Forever

### Words & Music by Brian May

Again, taken from the soundtrack of the film *Highlander*, set in the spectacular Scottish landscape, this song by Brian May frames poignant scenes in the film where Connor MacLeod cradles his dying wife Heather in his arms, realizing that, as an immortal who remains forever young, he will be without her for the rest of his time.

**Hints & Tips: Take your time with this song — the tempo is marked *rubato*, meaning you can play the song at your preferred pace and add your own expression.**

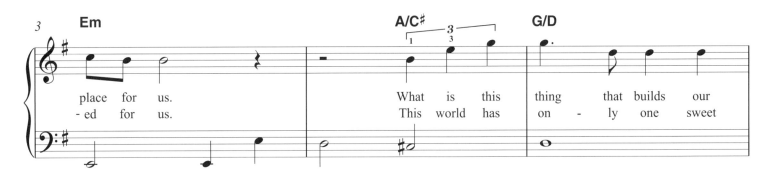

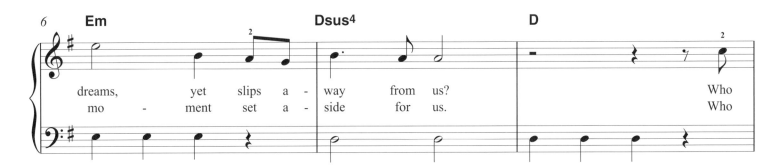

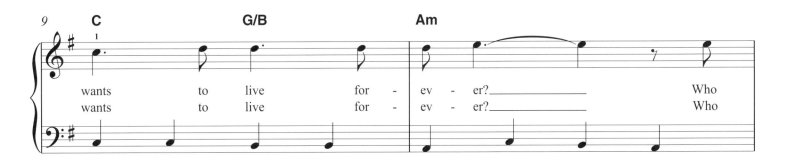

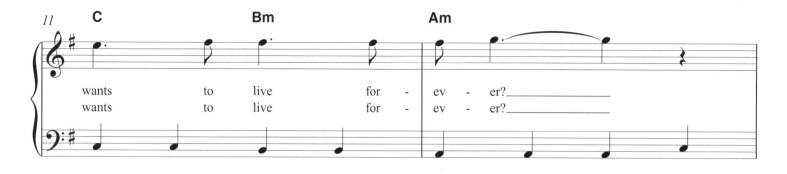

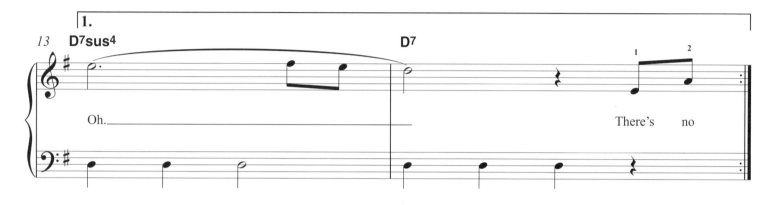

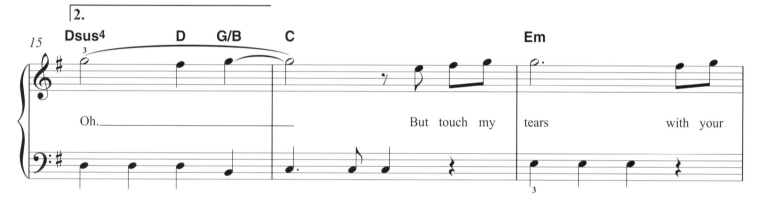

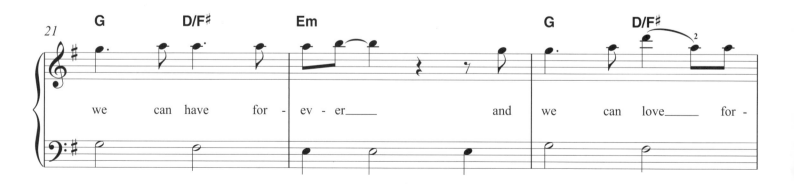

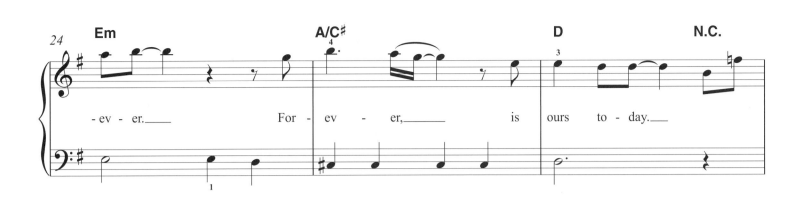

-ev - er.\_\_\_\_ For- ev - er,\_\_\_\_ is ours to - day.\_\_\_\_

Who wants to live for - ev - er?\_\_\_\_ Who

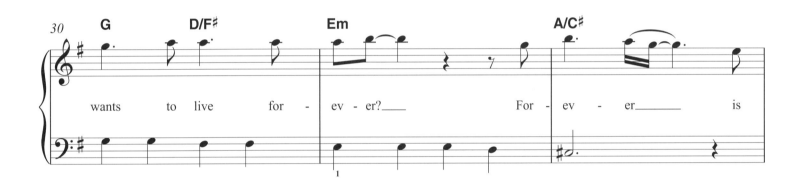

wants to live for - ev - er?\_\_\_\_ For - ev - er\_\_\_\_ is

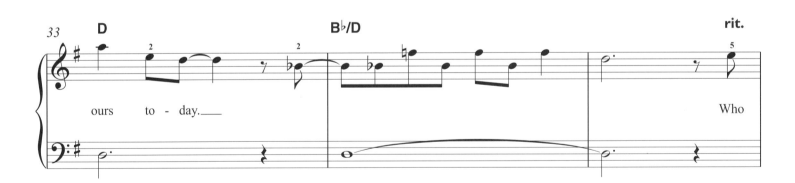

ours to - day.\_\_\_\_ Who

waits for - ev - er an - y - way?_____

# We Are The Champions

## Words & Music by Freddie Mercury

Of this anthemic power ballad, Freddie Mercury said: "I was thinking about football when I wrote it. I wanted a participation song, something the fans could latch on to." This certainly proved to be the case, as the song is still widely used to celebrate sporting victories and in 1994 was the official theme song for the *FIFA World Cup*.

**Hints & Tips:** Keep the left-hand arpeggios in the first half steady and flowing. Be aware of the key change in bar 18.

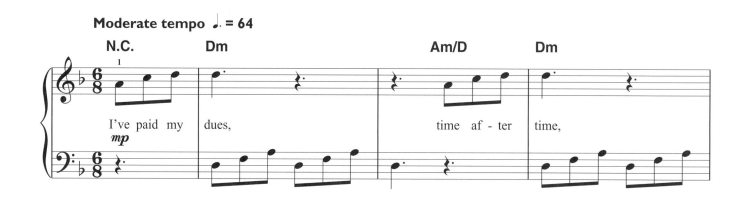

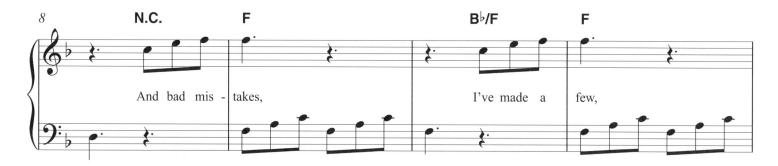

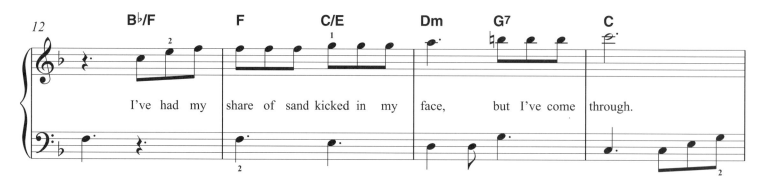

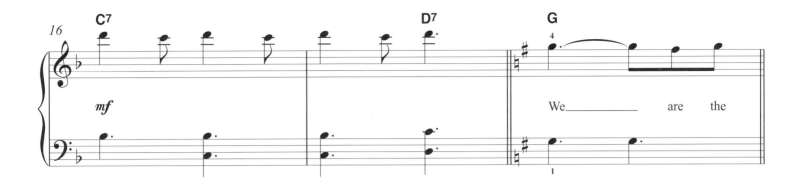

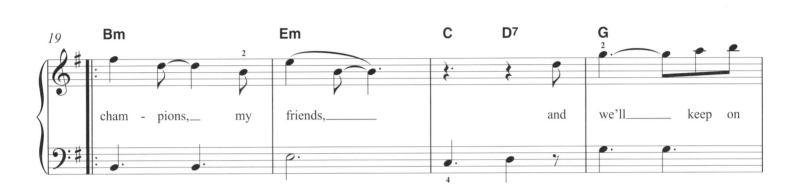

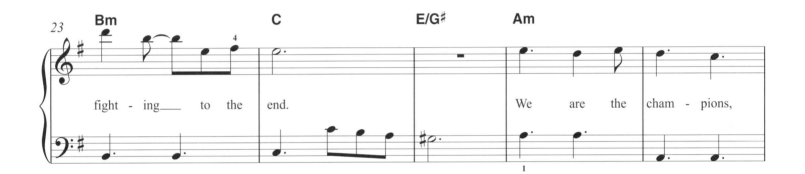

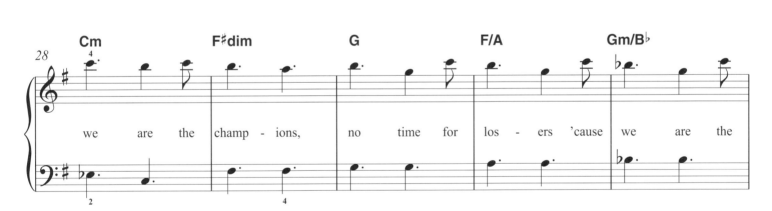

# We Will Rock You

**Words & Music by Brian May**

One of the most iconic Queen songs, 'We Will Rock You' was written by guitarist, Brian May, who had the intention of creating a song that could involve audience participation. It appears on their 1977 album, *News Of The World* and is followed by Freddie Mercury's track, 'We Are The Champions'. Because of this, the songs are usually played back to back — Queen would often end their live shows with both songs as a joint encore.

**Hints & Tips: Keep the left hand steady throughout this song to maintain the pulsing, driving feel of the song. This song isn't too fast — be sure not to rush the right-hand sixteenth notes.**

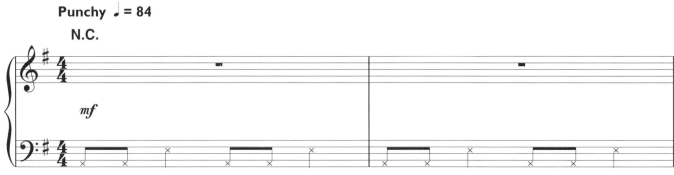

*Tap side of piano with left hand, alternate palm and knuckles*

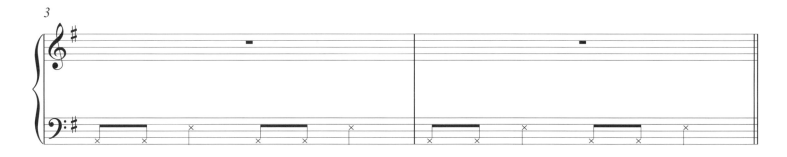

John - ny, you're a poor man, big man, play-ing in the street, gon - na be a big man some day.

Blood on your face, big dis - grace, kick - in' your can all o - ver the place, sing - in':

'We will, we will rock you.

*f*

We will, we will rock you.

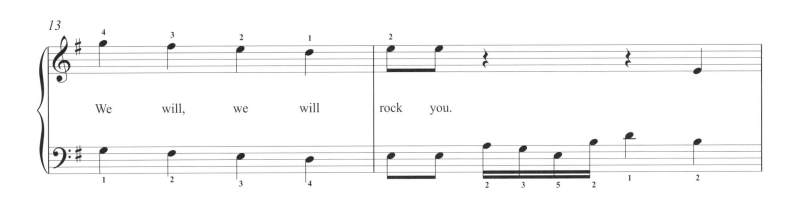

We will, we will rock you.

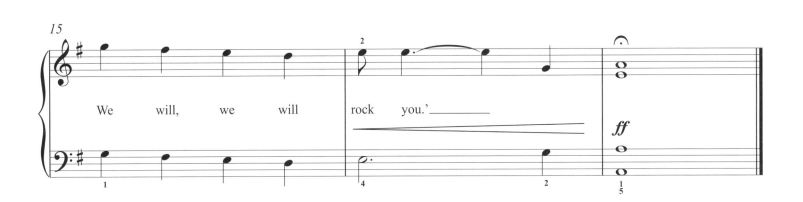

We will, we will rock you.'_____

*ff*

# You're My Best Friend

**Words & Music by John Deacon**

Following on from Bohemian Rhapsody, this was the second single to be released from the 1975 album *A Night At The Opera*. The ballad was written by bass guitarist John Deacon for his wife Veronica, whom he had married in January of that year, and became a popular contrast to the band's more usual rock-orientated style.

**Hints & Tips: This song has a swing feel. Use the quarter notes in the left hand to keep the beat steady and moving, but keep it light.**

**Moderate swing feel ♩ = 118**

Ooh, you make me live.___ What - ev - er this world can

give to me,___ it's you you're all I see.___

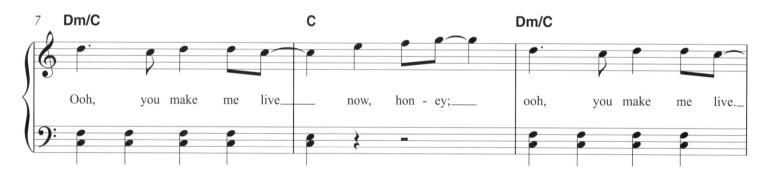

Ooh, you make me live___ now, hon - ey;___ ooh, you make me live._

Oh,___ you're the best friend that

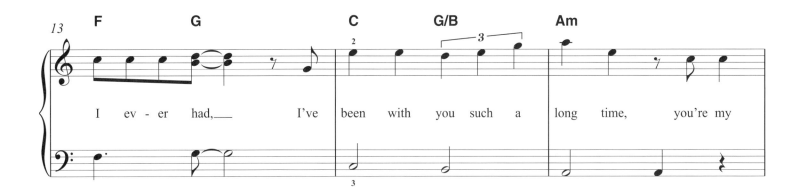

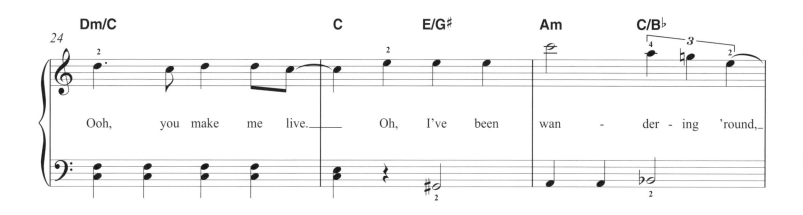

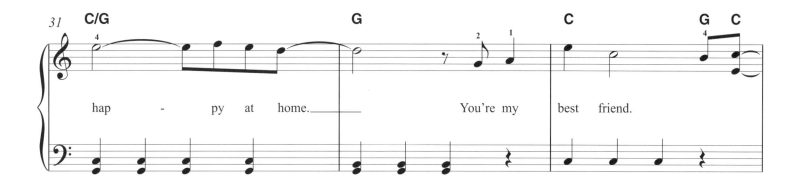

# It's Easy to Play Your Favorite Songs with Hal Leonard Easy Piano Books

### The Beatles Best – 2nd Edition

120 arrangements for easy piano, including: All My Loving • Dear Prudence • Eleanor Rigby • Good Day Sunshine • In My Life • Let It Be • Michelle • Ob-La-Di, Ob-La-Da • Revolution • Something • Yesterday • and more.

00231944 .............................. $24.99

### The Best Broadway Songs Ever

This bestseller features 80+ Broadway faves: All I Ask of You • I Wanna Be a Producer • Just in Time • My Funny Valentine • On My Own • Seasons of Love • The Sound of Music • Tomorrow • Younger Than Springtime • more!

00300178 .............................. $22.99

### The Best Praise & Worship Songs Ever

The name says it all: over 70 of the best P&W songs today. Titles include: Awesome God • Blessed Be Your Name • Come, Now Is the Time to Worship • Days of Elijah • Here I Am to Worship • Open the Eyes of My Heart • Shout to the Lord • We Fall Down • and more.

00311312 .............................. $19.99

### The Best Songs Ever

Over 70 all-time favorite songs, including: All I Ask of You • Body and Soul • Call Me Irresponsible • Edelweiss • Fly Me to the Moon • The Girl from Ipanema • Here's That Rainy Day • Imagine • Let It Be • Moonlight in Vermont • People • Somewhere Out There • Tears in Heaven • Unforgettable • The Way We Were • and more.

00359223 .............................. $19.95

Get complete song lists and more at
**www.halleonard.com**

*Pricess, contents, and availability subject to change without notice*
*Disney characters and artwork © Disney Enterprises, Inc.*

### First 50 Popular Songs You Should Play on the Piano

50 great pop classics for beginning pianists to learn, including: Candle in the Wind • Chopsticks • Don't Know Why • Hallelujah • Happy Birthday to You • Heart and Soul • I Walk the Line • Just the Way You Are • Let It Be • Let It Go • Over the Rainbow • Piano Man • and many more.

00131140 .............................. $16.99

### Jumbo Easy Piano Songbook

200 classical favorites, folk songs and jazz standards. Includes: Amazing Grace • Beale Street Blues • Bridal Chorus • Buffalo Gals • Canon in D • Cielito Lindo • Danny Boy • The Entertainer • Für Elise • Greensleeves • Jamaica Farewell • Marianne • Molly Malone • Ode to Joy • Peg O' My Heart • Rockin' Robin • Yankee Doodle • dozens more!

00311014 .............................. $19.99

### Best Children's Songs Ever – 2nd Edition

This amazing collection features 101 songs, including: Beauty and the Beast • Do-Re-Mi • Hakuna Matata • Happy Birthday to You • If I Only Had a Brain • Let It Go • On Top of Spaghetti • Over the Rainbow • Puff the Magic Dragon • Rubber Duckie • Winnie the Pooh • and many more.

00159272 .............................. $19.99

### 150 of the Most Beautiful Songs Ever

Easy arrangements of 150 of the most popular songs of our time. Includes: Bewitched • Fly Me to the Moon • How Deep Is Your Love • My Funny Valentine • Some Enchanted Evening • Tears in Heaven • Till There Was You • Yesterday • You Are So Beautiful • and more. 550 pages of great music!

00311316 .............................. $27.50

### 50 Easy Classical Themes

Easy arrangements of 50 classical tunes representing more than 30 composers, including: Bach, Beethoven, Chopin, Debussy, Dvorak, Handel, Haydn, Liszt, Mozart, Mussorgsky, Puccini, Rossini, Schubert, Strauss, Tchaikovsky, Vivaldi, and more.

00311215 .............................. $14.99

### Popular Sheet Music – 30 Hits from 2015-2017

30 songs: Burn • Cheap Thrills • City of Stars • Don't Wanna Know • HandClap • H.O.L.Y. • Love on the Weekend • Million Reasons • Ophelia • Ride • Say You Won't Let Go • 7 Years • Shape of You • This Town • When We Were Young • and more.

00233043 .............................. $17.99

### VH1's 100 Greatest Songs of Rock and Roll

The results from the VH1 show that featured the 100 greatest rock and roll songs of all time are here in this awesome collection! Songs include: Born to Run • Good Vibrations • Hey Jude • Hotel California • Imagine • Light My Fire • Like a Rolling Stone • Respect • and more.

00311110 .............................. $29.99

### Disney's My First Song Book

16 favorite songs to sing and play. Every page is beautifully illustrated with full-color art from Disney features. Songs include: Beauty and the Beast • Bibbidi-Bobbidi-Boo • Circle of Life • Cruella De Vil • A Dream Is a Wish Your Heart Makes • Hakuna Matata • Under the Sea • Winnie the Pooh • You've Got a Friend in Me • and more.

00310322 .............................. $16.99

HAL•LEONARD®